RAIN

RAIN

POEMS

HENRY CARLILE

CARNEGIE MELLON UNIVERSITY PRESS
PITTSBURGH 1994

ACKNOWLEDGMENTS

Grateful acknowledgment is made to the editors and publishers of the following publications in which these poems first appeared:

The American Poetry Review: "Another Low Dishonest Decade," "The Cloud and the Plow and the Meaning of Rhyme," "Desire," "In The Traveling Salesman's Wake" (under the title "Divorce"), "The Triangle."
Calapooya Collage: "Morning Song," "Vaux's Swifts."
Crazyhorse: "For a Fisherman," "Four Variations on the Invisible Bittern" (reprinted in *The Best of Crazyhorse*, University of Arkansas Press, 1990), "Mercy," "November Memo," "Singles Bar," "To a Journalist in Sweden," "Winter Raven, Summer Crow."
The Iowa Review: "Merlin."
Jeopardy: "Off Port Townsend, One Month Before the Arrival of the U.S.S. Ohio (first printed as a broadside by Sea Pen Press and Paper Mill and later anthologized in *The Pushcart Prize XI: Best of the Small Presses, 1986-1987 Ed.*, The Pushcart Press, 1986).
The Kentucky Poetry Review: "The Pigeons of Istanbul."
The Laurel Review: "The Girlfriend," "Hunting, Hazards and Holiness."
The Ohio Review: "Dead Reckoning."
Poetry: "Camouflage" (reprinted in the *Anthology of Magazine Verse and Yearbook of American Poetry, 1986-1987 Ed.*, Monitor Book Company, 1988), "In Oceans, in Rivers," "The Poet's Neighbor Talks Back."
Shenandoah: "The Death of Casanova," "Graveyard Shift," "Metamorphosis and Marriage," "Train Whistles in the Wind and Rain" (reprinted in *The Pushcart Prize XVII: Best of the Small Presses, 1992-1993 Ed.*, The Pushcart Press, 1992).
Tar River Poetry: "Fort Ord, California, 1953," "Her Things," "Instruments."

Thanks to the Ingram Merrill Foundation for their generous award of a grant that allowed me to complete many of these poems.

Special thanks also to Tess Gallagher and Lee VanDemarr for their responses to these poems in manuscript.

Publication of this book is supported by a grant from the Pennsylvania Council on the Arts.

Library of Congress Catalog Card Number 93-73476
ISBN 0-88748-166-3
ISBN 0-88748-167-1 Pbk.

Printed and bound in the United States of America

10 9 8 7 6 5 4 3 2 1

Contents

I

In Oceans, In Rivers   11
Desire   13
Fort Ord, California, 1953   14
To a Journalist in Sweden   16
Camouflage   17
Dead Reckoning   18
Another Low Dishonest Decade   20
Off Port Townsend, One Month Before the Arrival
                                of the U.S.S. Ohio   21

II

The Death of Casanova   25
The Girlfriend   27
Triangle   28
In the Traveling Salesman's Wake   30
Singles Bar   31
The Poet's Neighbor Talks Back   32
Four Variations on the Invisible Bittern   34
Metamorphosis and Marriage   36
The Pigeons of Istanbul   37
Morning Song   38
Her Anger   39
Her Things   40

III

The Cloud and the Plow and the Meaning of Rhyme   43
Hunting, Hazards, and Holiness   44
Vaux's Swift   46
Winter Raven, Summer Crow   48

IV

November Memo	61
Instruments	62
Graveyard Shift	64
Mercy	65
For a Fisherman	68
Merlin	74
Train Whistles in the Wind and Rain	75

in memoriam
CARL MORRIS

I

Hour after hour they ponder the warm field—
And the far valley behind, where the buttercup
Had blessed with gold their slow boots coming up,
Where even the little brambles would not yield,
But clutched and clung to them like sorrowing hands;
They breathe like trees unstirred.

—WILFRED OWEN

Over brine reaches the flat rounds fall.
Cannons to raise the dead, Mark Twain?
It makes no sense to say they
rise to reports they lived by,
corrupt finally in the ocean's peacock eyes,
their own eyes kissed out by fish.

These have not risen. They race
along grave sunken avenues tides make,
gassing up for the long ascent through
green panes of light, through diatomaceous
snows and the slowly pulsing blooms of
blue jellies, lost parachutists of the deeps.

Astern, our dragged lines bend in rips
that toll low warnings from the entrance bell.
We hope no more than fish,
no bent back and downward streaming hair
like seaweed when the sea drains from rocks,
no death that calls us to ourselves.

*

A suicide once drifted toward my line,
spinning slowly in the frigid river,
his black humped back dipping and rising
as from an unpurged habit of love.

It was May, at the peak of the spring
salmon run, with cherry trees in bloom.
Suspended from school for fighting,
my glasses broken, I squinted
and saw death's gradual turning blur,

black four-pronged star, divining
my rod down, singing my reel
to its clicking mass.

When my line snapped free and slack,
retightening in the current, I knew
how the dead bite, hang on to what
they keep, then don't, then slip away.

This is the story I told a friend once
who asked why poets write
so much about death and
why not just go fishing instead.

DESIRE

> The president stares out at me from the stove,
> more wrinkled than ever where I have
> tucked him with the usual hopes for peace
> and the latest forecast of the economy.
>
> In one of the meditations you have to imagine
> the object of your desire as her face blisters
> and falls apart, the skull is what you're after.
> You meditate on that, you think of fire.
>
> Fire is a bad rhyme and good remedy for desire.
> Imagine the skull in the flames parted from
> its face flown up the chimney.
> As that poor old couple in Eudora Welty's story
>
> burned the furniture one winter night.
> Because they had worked all their lives.
> Because they had nothing but a few plants
> and a house they couldn't call their own.
>
> Outside, the freeze-warning whistle blew and blew
> first for the plants and then for them.
> The president, if he wants, can set every whistle
> in this country blowing, he can freeze your heart.
>
> All the same, I pause before I light the match,
> superstitious about symbols but clear enough
> to think burning the president is no answer.
> Forgive me Sir, I say, my house is cold.

Fort Ord, California, 1953

1.
Conscientious Objector

Through dust deepened by others
we practiced to be missed,
cursing, an olive-green flotsam,
venomous and terrified.

Through smoke from mock bombs,
through the flare's blue failing light,
like amputees on knees and elbows,
with M-1's crooked in our arms,

beneath thorns of barbed wire
and the stitched red lines of bullets
we rowed our flesh against earth
and made slow progress.

Then one more desperate than the rest
put up his hand and howled
and fell back clutching his wrist,
the rags where fingers had flexed.

We knew the truce would soon be signed.
Touch that had fathomed Preludes
protested to the dust. For what?
There will be other wars, he said.

2.
Stell

We have learned how to march backward
and meet ourselves coming home
in a rubber bag.
And Stell put his hand up as though
to stop that other war and took
a thirty-caliber machine gun bullet
through the fingers of his right hand.

I was twenty feet away and lay for fear
with an M-1 pressed against my cheek,
screaming Cease fire! Cease fire!
as tracers snapped above my head
and Panmunjom waited to be news.

Stell was chickenshit, the sergeant said,
stirring coffee in the mess, and told
the KPs how he'd fried a North Korean near
Choisin with a white phosphorus grenade.
Man, the shit burns through you,
you should've heard him scream.

The others couldn't stand it.
I blew his head off with a BAR.
But that dumb fucker Stell, remember
how he played that longhair shit
on the day room piano? Drove me nuts.

There was no poetry between us, only politics and prose.
But Sweden has a yellow and blue flag I was curious about.
We were great to get away from out there on the Baltic
where I thought of Martinson and Tranströmer and Bly
like a flea on a surfboard jigging for the deep image.

We were sailing to Åland, the nearest Finnish possession,
but as I leaned over the rail into an existential haze
(and this was months before your navy discovered it)
I imagined a Russian submarine scattering the herring
from their rendezvous with new potatoes and akvavit.

Past worn gray archipelagos and the sad turrets
of many-millimetered guns guarding the straits
the Silja ferry brought us back to Stockholm.
But that was no home for me, morosely Bergmanesque,
gathering intelligence from failed intentions.

On the plane to London I thought fondly of you
still banging the keys, my sweet unmusical Marxist,
spelling it all out in prose like burnt rubber.
The best you could do, I thought, back on the ground,
sipping bitters in Heathrow before the next flight out.

Back home in America, I recalled Midsummer's Eve
near Öregrund, or was that somewhere else? That night
when something surfaced and blew the water from its throat.
I think it breathed to charge itself, I think it felt
responsible for lives it might be called to account for.

From the beach the rocks I hurled fell short,
gave back no flash of extinguished life.
I was mad at it, at you, at me mostly.
If what was out there heard me, it gave no sign, being
sworn to secrecy, restraint of its huge inhuman grief.

CAMOUFLAGE

On the door it says what to do to survive
But we were not born to survive
Only to live
                    —W. S. Merwin

So many piles of leaves are walking about these days
disguised as humans it must give pause.
Originally we meant only to fool ducks, dupe deer
into posing like St. Sebastian, but now it looks
like we are hiding from other heaps that mean harm,
that mean to steal us from our families and lovers
or steel us against the unhappy prospect of quaking
like so many aspens in the arms of winter.

Or is it simply that we mean to advertise a sincere
wish to become one with nature and quietly disappear
toting our taped and silenced M-16's and Mini-14's
and other automatic acronyms of extreme prejudice?
There is big business in camouflage these days.
We can be anything we want to be at last!
A summer wood, an autumn wood, a big beige desert.
We can even be dead grass, we can be snow.
And let me not fail to mention our latest fashion,
Night. Night is very popular these days.

What we do not want to be is colorful, color is
suspect, a thing of the past, except for a week or
maybe two weeks in spring, during the spring offensives,
when even the desert forgets itself and laughs floridly.
Then it is safe to be a field of poppies.

But we must never forget the latest heat-seeking
technologies that have kept pace with our trade.
Telescopes so powerful they are capable of detecting,
at incredible distances in the coldest environments,
the small trembling heart of a mouse, o soldiers of
fortune and misfortune, they mean to find us out,
to discover in our iciest resolve a spot of warmth.

When I first heard of it I thought of counting casualties
after a battle with scraps of paper blowing
over the battlefield and the dead already stiffening
into postures of poisoned insect larvae, the pockets
of their mud-encrusted uniforms turned out, their weapons
like broken-off antennae.
                                        Or else it seemed as in
some archaeological dig after a great calamity, removed
in time, in which the dead, long ossified, were given
numbers in place of names.

Now I see it refers to navigation, a way of plotting
the safest course from A to B defined in way points,
through dangerous shoals revealed at ebb, concealed
at flood by tidal rips.
                                But fog renders dead reckoning
largely futile since distinguishing landmarks
are required such as, say, a lighthouse or island
or distant radio or television tower on some hill.
Which vessel, lacking any view of same, must proceed
with caution utilizing compass and fathometer,
plotting time and tidal currents combined with knots
and distance traveled and hope that wind or other
variables have not compromised the plotted course.

Even here the first impression holds.
One sees the drowned faces drifting with lethal
floral jellies—dull oranges, ghostly blues—
and the upthrust masts of a trawler come to grief,
stuck crookedly from shallows, marker on an ancient
grave, half its crewmen saved to wash against
some other shore in the dead heat or cold of day or night,
where rumpled hospital sheets recall a line of breakers
to be crossed before the fever ebbs and one floats on
the harbor's mirror, its reflected masts and lights.

The sailor beached but not yet soundly asleep remembers
latitudes beyond this present harbor where
tonnages foundered and went down like marriages:
here a deep-sea-going tug, there a freighter or tanker,
and always the smaller craft, unheedful of storm warnings,
gone out like sea-blown swarms of fireflies—ephemeral
pleasure crafters, sport fishermen—gone.

But the retired master, torpedoed twice in the North
Atlantic, must hear his own heart's S.O.S. on the sickroom
monitor and recall the cries of drowned shipmates,
the darkness building above his bed like that
typhoon off Malaya, or was it Singapore, in 1932 or 3,
when half the fleet went down, the water like a long
deferred annuity, congestive, rising in his lungs.
Half delirious, he spies the ferryman
 rowing patiently toward shore.

To the ferryman, it's poor business, the one-way fare,
the journey from the island profitless.
Still he rows, having nothing else to do, toward
that cargo moored to its monitor, waiting to off load.
And the master, who once commanded a flagship,
remembers a model of the Constitution sailing
in a bottle and fears the approaching shallows,
that white shore where his own hands,
mutinous, stray indifferent to his commands.

ANOTHER LOW DISHONEST DECADE

These are the intervals when
even the strong lose faith,
indulge in prayer and believe
the platitudes of those who
bear themselves like afterbirth
through the chambers of justice
and the thoroughfares.

Off Port Townsend, One Month Before the Arrival of the U.S.S. Ohio

Down Haro Strait and the Strait of Juan De Fuca
the killer whales would breach and roll,
lifting tall dorsals free of the water, breath
popping like steam valves on old boilers.
Black and white they were, like a giant string quartet.

Not vicious as we'd thought,
but tamable and captive, aiming only to please.
Once lonely sailors rocked from sleep
by their music through a ship's hull
mistook them for mermaids.

Now, if you put your ear to the water
you might listen to the hiss of electrons,
the turbine's deep nuclear hum,
and pulse of propellers at each revolution
whispering no to the hope of cities.

The morning I saw my first Poseidon
I forgot the salmon I had come to fish for
and rammed the throttle open, closing
at twenty knots, quartering on its bow,
my ragged ban-the-Trident flag unfurled.

From their high place surrounded by periscopes
the curious officers looked down.
I was no Bogart, my boat no African Queen.
I only wished to keep this Poseidon safe
in some post-nuclear museum,
a tame nose we might pat
disarming as the whale's, but for now
it holds course through reaches darkened
by its pace, staining the scenery
it slips through like grease.

Tacking from that wake, I bore toward a reef
of gulls and auklets, candlefish and rising salmon,
white sand cliffs where madronas start and whisper,
blue sky, a red bell hanging on slack tide,
the only black, exposed rock, the whale's dorsal.

Once there was a city state that promised everything,
white as the sand cliffs, with olive trees, promenades
framed in marble, and statues of the old, cruel gods.
Poseidon was one, his weapon the trident—names
we thought we could use because they meant nothing.

II

. . . love cannot exist divided.
In love's nature, two functions as one,
and there is ardor, willing, and longing.

—ECKHART

Only in the lurid fluorescence of his office
could she see how aged he was, and bored.
In the brandy-light of bars his face retained
its youthful aquiline but dangerous beauty.

And sometimes while they made love,
through the whole of a weekend afternoon,
his face, flushed with effort, approaching
and withdrawing, seemed ageless.

Now in a hearse he rides, drawn by seven
geldings to his final liaison, having learned
in searching for the Other there would always
be another, nothing left but his legacy:

the last classically restrained
but lewd memoirs of a roué who made
seduction his religion—disciplined
in its variations on the one theme.

So he who could lie with anyone now lies
chaste in death, a rose for company
left by a woman of that name, whose favors,
purchased not by artifice but with coin,

required only this skill, an ability
to read, albeit without understanding,
while clothed only in underthings,
a tale too boring for words.

His head drooped, his eyes closed,
a drop of spittle hung from his lip,
his hands, soft as a woman's but speckled
like trout, locked together as in prayer.

Then she would leave, having covered him
where he snored, an ancient pale doll,
his breath sour as the wind from a sump.
Casanova, in his comforter, in California.

Bury him beneath palms, within earshot
of the shore where women, naked and numerous,
stalk the white sands and recall him, if
they recall him, as fatherly and obscure.

Once she took a knife
from the rack
and meant to use it.

Drop it! I said,
pinning her wrist
against the sink.

You have to suffer it
anyway, you may as well
wait for the end.

Live or die amounts
to the same thing.
It's boring! she said.

Well then, stab me,
I told her releasing her
wrist, not meaning it.

And by God she did.
I have the scar.
She, of course, is gone.

In the manner of Giacometti,
whom she admired, she sculpted
as part of her graduate study
three figures plastered together,
two women with a man between.

One of the women shared
a common leg with the man,
like a Siamese twin's.
The third figure's were her own.
Alive, she might have walked away.

The sculptor, who walked
when she was done, left it
for others to wonder at.
At the end of the art department
hallway it stood for years.

A whirling struggle of arms
and legs all pulling
in opposite directions,
scarred with student graffiti
and chipped and scratched by

the janitor's cleaning tools,
who must have cursed it as
an obstacle to a tidier
life of bare hallways
and gleaming floors.

One of the professors,
his name escapes me,
would on occasion stand
before it as though
confused by its appearance.

Nothing to do with problems
of balance and perspective
that must have troubled
the sculptor. She had
named it *The Triangle*.

I know too little of art
to venture how good it was.
I only know that one day
for some reason or other
it was put out in the trash.

And you could see clear
to the end of the hallway
it had stood in and out
a window to the parking lot
across the street.

Like a hired hand with Alzheimer's
he drifts back to the homestead
and can't recall the former owners,
although the scene is vaguely familiar.
Absently he cranks the handle
that raises water from the well
and brings up a bucket slimed
with dead mosquito larvae,
and drinks, drinks until
his head clears.

The barn stood there,
and where those stumps are, the orchard.
There the windmill, and there
the three silos, and beyond that
the house from which his wife once
called him in for dinner.
Nothing remains from what she burned
behind her when she left.
That arbor, gone now in a riot of weeds,
was her undoing where, in grape shadow,
she waited, unpinning her braids.

But he is back to cultivate,
to raise the new barn and house
and plant trees and nurture back
whatever else she ruined
before she left,
lured off by a gigolo
in a loud suit.

That one's face hangs like meat on a hook,
and the one next to him turns blearily to ask
What do they want anyway? Tenderness, my
daughter said against a boyfriend who had none.
Kindness, my wife said closing her book.
In this place we cure, divorced, separated,
learning by degrees, by percentages and proofs,
by turns of cheek both tender and tough.

But some hurt by too long reflection stare
into the mirrors of glasses, of bottles neatly
lined in rows repeating the same grievance
with their bent spouts, their shades of amber.
And one, finding the atmosphere too dark, strays
into the afternoon and horns of stalled traffic.

THE POET'S NEIGHBOR TALKS BACK

I haven't her cleverness with words
but nevertheless hope to convince you,
whatever else she might have said,
I'm not the nature-destroying villain
my neighbor portrays me as but rather
a loving and responsible husband and father.
Though my ex-wife is bound to disagree.

True, as my neighbor says in one poem,
I chain-sawed the cherry tree and,
by a miscalculation of the undercut
she ought not be expected to understand,
felled the cherry smack on the birdbath.
Not, as she implies, intentionally,
but the birdbath was unfortunately ruined.

And it's true I dug up the forsythia
and the mums my wife had planted
(then let fall face down in mud),
and I removed also other ornamentals
whose roots had threatened to undermine
the foundation of our house. But my neighbor,
would she fathom *that* sort of foundation, ever?

Or realize I'd planned to replace
those plants with more manageable species,
pleasing to the eye, that might have
inspired more loving, less judgmental
response from her, had she been so inclined?
I was hurt by her poem, need I say, because
for eighteen years we'd been good neighbors.

And I had been her friend even after
I saw her coming home with a strange man,
a flushed, happy smile on her face
and her arms full of wildflowers, while
her garden, like my wife's, went to seed.
And I said nothing to her husband, it being
after all, none of my business what she did.

Soon after this, she and her husband divorced,
and yesterday, thinking back, I recalled that
unfortunate man—whom I incidentally liked—
in their last year of marriage kneeling
in the garden she'd planted that spring,
pulling the weeds she'd let grow there.
And I heard rumors he'd taken to drink.

Under the circumstances, who could blame him?
But he did nothing, I'm sorry to say, about
the dandelions on their lawn, and as the seeds
were not contained by the fence that divides
these properties, I now have their drift
to contend with. And one more thing I forgot
to mention: The tree I cut down was dead.

All morning I searched for the right decoy,
wanting a bittern in its reedlike pose,
but found only mallards, wood ducks, teal,
canvasbacks, old squaws, scaups,
a lovely ruddy duck already spoken for,
whistling swans, Canada geese
and one magnificent, unaffordable loon.
Always we settle for less.

Instead I bought you a pied-billed grebe,
recalling its mating song
heard on the walks we used to take
by Reed College pond
where we saw the green heron
but no bittern.

*

Unlikely now together we will ever see one.
Before we married, the bitterns I observed
and later wrote about were seldom paired.
Before one flushed from cover I might see
only an eye reflective and wary.

Sixteen and curious as Audubon to know
how rushes gathered into something
birdlike and flew away,
I'm ashamed to admit I shot one.
It fell like a spent bag of change.

Its outraged yellow eye seemed to accuse me.
But why exaggerate? It was a dead bird.
Audubon had killed his share to better purpose:
dead models stiffly painted live.

*

And carefully you wrote of what you had seen only
in photographs, in taxidermed and dusty glass-eyed
specimens, habitats of unnatural history museums.
More stately and serious, years later and older,
the ghost bird lived from your lines and flew.

Though not as I had seen it through swamp vapors,
over the water-ferned and cattailed green margins
of hidden ponds, Venetian scenery of spring meadows,
unlikely in flight as one of those post da-Vincian
manned contraptions that always crashed.

The bittern somehow airborne, dipping and weaving,
gathered straight down into a stillness,
in semblance of rushes, matched their swaying,
betrayed only by its eye's flavescent yellow.

*

You wrote once you could go blindly on
loving a life from which something is missing.
I never read those lines and believed
it was the bittern you meant.

Say bitterns appear like grace to the fallen and
bitter, the solitary souls who step through loss
without hope of discovery, without leaving a trace.

Say now your life is singular (even if it's not)
that you find those rarely observed features,
that starry pupil refined into a tangible self-
hood, a temperature several degrees above human.

I want that bird to show itself to you.
Eighteen years you were my best and wisest friend.
I never wanted to be what is missing.

We are exposed to what we are supposed to be.
It goes on like this for years and goes on.
As if we hadn't guessed the danger in small subsistence,
the imperative of change because of the harm we could
do each other and ourselves if we didn't. It wasn't
desertion we intended, more like the fawn that lies
so still it becomes a part of the scene, the inscape
of its fearful self a vast and dangerous country
where loss of camouflage brings grief.

You wore your morning colors as though unaware
of approaching twilight and the limousines or hearses
pressing through the gates, past the stone lion
and the stone bull and the ugly fountains called
Charity and Belief. A hydra's hydrants, so many
mouths speaking indirectly in a certain way
their voices trickled to a contrived order.

Not that either of us believed in that spotty
protection bent spiritually in circular designs.
The patterns seemed to shift into each other at times
so reflections wore spots or the spots seemed reflective.
And we believed they changed. They *did* change.
And we also, less tangibly out of place than out
of the scene we had banked on so carefully, through
charity and belief each wanting to come out spotless
and secretly understanding how impossible that was.

Not quite innocent she approaches
over white sand where ocean blooms
and delays its rupture and spill,
brown hair I love
caught in the wind's whirl.

I've placed her on the mantel
between two candles, image
memory must enlarge to re-embrace,
American, unconverted by muezzins
wailing from their minarets.

In Istanbul, devout and dusty city
where she lives, far from this ocean
and familiar shore, she wakes
in her husband's bed to that wailing,
fundamentally adored.

As Rilke said, "guiltless, guilty"
in the mortal pose of Eve, she keeps
close counsel as she combs her hair.
While pigeons, forever free and godless,
circle through the morning prayer.

I love to watch her as she rakes her hair,
dragging its darkness through the comb,
swearing under her breath when something
catches, and something in the way she tilts
her head and tosses it to shake her mane
and spill it shining down her back reminds
me of another, years ago, her opposite with
lighter hair, who loved and helped me when
I could not help myself. But she is gone.
And this one I love, here so late! so late!
will reap refinement of my trial and error,
that others have paid for, and paid dearly.
It's only fair unless I tell myself it isn't,
upbraiding myself as she braids her hair.

Her Anger

She is the keeper of my hands, those nervous pickers,
my garrulous, bright-beautiful, quiet only when I cover her.
She rides her horse bareback, bareassed down
to the river with its swelling of stars and drinks
on her knees, hair weeping into the current
that is always pulling us back to the sea.
The hidden stones blur up at her, then clear,
then blur in the ancient language of eddies.
She's who I have waited for, must love,
though her tongue abrades like a cat's tongue, and
her eyes, hard bearings tempered in the brightness of
heat, do not forgive until I touch—I who always fear it—
and touch again the rejecting contours, forgiving
fissures, and she turns and says, You're so thoughtless, and . . .

Scarf here, blouse there, and now this shoe tipped
beside the bed like a kayak holed in the bow.
The madcap ship of fashion passed this undulant
square island and left these in its wake: hairbrush,
hairs, panties on the exercycle, bra on the doorknob,
water glass, hand cream, book of criticism scribbled
full of objections (nightly soporific stronger than
pills), jewelry, lipstick, one button loose
from somewhere like a snout from its pig, purse
extruding tissue, tickets, pennies, nickels, quarters,
feathered mask—my pheasant!—from the Halloween ball.
Once there were shadows on these walls where paintings
had hung, the dusty outline of a missing dresser.
Once this bedroom was empty before she filled it.

III

*Mr. Gurdjieff told me that in some schools they
could, by special methods, make a sheep conscious.
But it just remained a conscious sheep. I asked him
what they did with it, and he said they ate it.*

—P. D. OUSPENSKY

You think the cloud will come closer and make
everything clear, that's what you think.
But it is elsewhere making someone else rain.
The man in the cloud-colored suit cannot undertake
his own shadow, it follows like a dog of rhyme.

He puts out the light and he is everywhere,
a shadow in the shadows, he turns on the light,
his shadow starts from him like gray business.
Why did you start this enterprise of rain?
The reasons for rhyme are everywhere.

You were not thinking of unplowing the fields.
You'd like the furrows to refrain
like a concentration of exact foreheads
all nodding as one—the bell calling every man
to mass on the same note, an absolute

disaster! Grief that embezzles and runs
spending from rill to rill, bringing on blades,
helping the hogs that pour from their pens
and your own pet grasshopper. All new!
And yet there is some precedent for this.

As after great thunder and sin you feel refreshed.
As after hard rain you see the steam rising
from fields and hear the birds starting up
all over again, their fierce little engines.
Strange you even knew they could sing.

Now they to their slogged forthwendings tend,
four hunters, guns askew like four unruly hairs,
to start the rabbit or pheasant from hiding.
But these cocks, wily, lie close and spy from
covert or culvert the passing grim party
and the rabbit keeps Viet-Cong-like to its digs.
Here is no hunting horn and gargle of hounds
among horse whinny and hoof stamp and ladies
in smart hunting habits, though these four
sport red in patterns motley or checkered and
in hues fluorescent as road crewmen's vests.
Small wonder the game is not game,
so uncouthly strikes the eye this drawling
troupe of unshaven hope and choler and color.

The roadside sparrows, come to dust, scatter
before the headlong hum of him leather-crouched,
helmet-missled over the speed-stretched oval
wheels of his hundred-mile-per-hour crotch rocket
all the way to Lone Tree past the six-foot
Iowa corn, surprised cows and hogs and the high
horse considering gravely over the fence this
black burst of boots and gloves and goggles.
So the goggle-eyed frog dives under a
scum of ditch-vetched water fern and the
blue-backed kestrel stoops from its crystal
insulator perch and, gray as a piece of the
paving, up springs the four-inch grasshopper
splat! like a nicotine bullet in the teeth.

Bearded buggy dads on their way to market,
fine trotters high-stepping between shafts,
broad-brim-hatted, blue-chambray-shirted,
with black pants and black suspenders, sons

like scrubbed minor replicas, dutiful
daughters, eyes downcast among chatter
of bonneted grannies and mothers, patriarchal
grandfathers observing that rain must come
as it always has, God's will be done, and
brief gossip also among the elders of shunning
a deacon caught in unnatural circumstances
with a pig—the Devil's own vessel!—and of
Sister Sara, who's soon to require the midwife,
as the moon too is full almost.

Vaux's Swifts

It began at dusk, a huge circling
that went on for fifteen minutes or more,
light failing, birds gathering from
miles around—such a storm of wings!

As if on signal, a funnel formed, probing
downward, darkening as it tightened,
descending toward our neighbor's house.
Inside, the TV burned through curtains

with news of other lives gone up in smoke.
While the bird wind, undetected, fell like
a cloud of cinders on high-speed film
reversed, sucked back down the chimney.

Inside, our neighbors slept, still unaware
of the hundreds of small beating hearts
inside their chimney; when we asked
next day, they hadn't heard a peep.

Good thing we didn't start a fire!
But the following afternoon,
before dusk when the gathering would
begin, the smoke rose from their chimney.

And here and there a swift circled,
as if lost, the flock
spread out for miles
like an orphanage evicted.

Where they slept that night is mystery.
We'd left our own fireplace unkindled,
hoping they'd favor us again.
But they were gone.

We didn't need the bird shit down our flue,
our neighbor said, plausible enough.
Better it seemed to us than a darker fear
of life too proximate in the night.

Winter Raven, Summer Crow

Huge, a raven
        launched off
a snow-burdened
             winter fir
stands croaking
    in the crystal glitter.

Head cocked
       right then left
  he watches as
            snowshoed we pass.

Sky thing
       fallen here,
  day creature
            night-shadowed
cobalt as
    his cousin crow.

Something's lost
      when suddenly
  he floats toward
           his remote roost.
Gray snag
      or promontory
  from which once
           and once only
the far bell
      of his cry
  claps back.

The cinder-tinted
      crow is curious,
    watching from
          a power line
as I hose the car.

The sponge glides
        over the hood
    spending its suds,
                intricate thousands
of bubbles iri-
        descent as
    light from feathers,
                a currency false
to him.

Haw! he laughs
        with his whole body,
    jiggling the wire,
                Haw! Haw!
a three-note
        warning as
    wings open
                him downwind,
umbrella-like
        blown from sight.

Absence of crows
        and ravens scarcifies,
    the suburban urn
                of wit emptied.
Cummerbunded
        summer robins
    scavenging earthworms
                from our gardening
do not suffice,
        nor tit cheeping
    in the laurel's
                winter gloom.

Reclusive raven,
     gregarious crow,
  in full day
         their midnight,
in lieu of music
    their carrion hue
  and cry.

*

I had a friend,
    a one-time poet,
  whose early verse
       recalled Rimbaud
and Crane and Thomas,
    only less so.
  Henry, he said,
     drunk, not on words,
in this business
    crows are commonplace,
  ravens scarce.
      So give up poetry,
he raved, strutting
    and preening himself.

You were my friend,
   inspiring
  as you discouraged,
      until urging less
for others con-
    demned you to
  the same advice.

I wish you were
        still bellowing
    from wine-stained,
                crossed-out pages
in the Blue Moon,
        where Roethke went,
    and James Wright,
                and Al Wiles
the wild painter
        leapt on a table
    shouting, *I have
                given the world
too much beauty!*

When a syndicate
        bought the Moon,
    and the bartender,
                high on meth,
laid fists on us
        and threw us out,
    it was past time
                to leave, the words
for once shamed
        out of us.
    Now gone separate ways,
                we never meet.

*

In Roethke's class,
          propping your arms
     on the table,
               flaunting your slashed
and bandaged wrists,
          your poems already
 sprouting into print
               like hammered lead
flowers, you seemed
          more poet even
     than he roaring
               from the table's end,
more widely read
     in the metaphysics that
obsessed you:
               Thomas Aquinas
and Eckhart, *The Secret
     of the Golden Flower*,
The Cloud of Unknowing.
               That shelf of books
your wife said
          was your undoing.

I can't see how.

*And insomuch thou
     shouldest be more meek
 and loving to thy
               ghostly spouse,
that He would meek him
     unto thee.*

But neither to a
        ghostly nor an
    earthly spouse
                could you meek yourself.
Nor to anyone.
        Not to sly Harold,
    your closest friend,
                a would-be Jesuit
become disciple of
        De Sade, who shared
    his Spanish gypsy
                wife with everyone,
if he could watch,
        and who answered the door
    naked, zucchini
                up his ass
and fed to friends
        that night for dinner.
    Wicked Harold,
                who went to England,
finally, and became
        a barrister.
    Not to any
        of a steady round
    of others:
                Fleshly janglers,
open praisers and blamers,
        tellers of trifles,
    ronners and tattlers
                of tales, and all
manner of pinchers
        who gathered at
    your table to snatch
                scraps of your wit.

Words wasted,
        wine spilled
   in the gothic-vaulted
                  dining room
   lit by candlelight
        and decorated
   in a neo-classic
                  neo-romantic
   hodgepodge of arti-
        facts oddly
   become baroque.

The women you scythed
        through like a blade
   through wheat and even
                  brought home
   to the marriage bed,
        telling your
   pretty wife
                  Move over!
   all deserted you.

But maybe one
        remembers you
   as a mad Jack
                  of her past
   who dared do anything
        but write.

Give up poetry?
        Too many ways
  to give it up.
            When it comes to us
at night begging
        our care, during
  lectures when we
                can't stop lecturing,
or just when we
        are walking nowhere
  with no pen
                or paper or even
a scrap of lead
        from a bullet
  to scribble it.

Death, we spoke
        too much of that.
  Whether a bullet
                might be better
than a pill
        or a knife along
  the wrist (your way)

                Death by drowning,
death by falling.

And I can't forget
        the intern sued
  because he missed
                a shard of glass
from the broken bottle
        in your leg.
  Money that kept you
                drunk for weeks.

Malpractice, when you
        so foully practiced
    on yourself the self-
                destruction you
believed might maim you
        into poetry.

How many nights
        you played for profit
    in your own country
                and wrote nothing.
The followers
        who came all hours
    to eat your words
                and swill your liquor
read little
        and cared less
    what you wrote.

As for poetry,
        years I've wanted
    to ignore your voice
                hoarse with drink
croak, Give it up!
    Jack, the pity
    that you did.

                        *

Somewhere there is
        a forest and in
    that forest a hemlock—
                not Socrates'

but another kind
        that taller, darker,
    has perspective
        a raven might
            appropriate.
    Not Poe's or yours,
    although it was
                your chosen totem.

It never croaks
        a Nevermore!
    as in Nevermore
                write poetry.
Or *Jamais plus*
        from the French
    translation by
                Baudelaire.

It has nothing to do
        with us and yet
    has something to do
                with poetry,
    being wise
        and solitary.

Like a black bell
        it sometimes clonks
    high in its hemlock
                steeple before
    the long glide
        home to its roost.

IV

Shall I say good morning while it is still night?
—SHUNTARŌ TANIKAWA

Something is happening to the pumpkin.
This morning, sweeping leaves away
from the front step, I noticed it.
The face that smiled foolishly at little
witches, goblins, Darth Vaders and E.T.s
is caving in beneath the green stem
of its barely visible beret, as though
deprived of interior light, an audience,
it had nothing else to say, would,
if it had hands, simply wave good-bye
and joke, *Thus runs the world away.*

On the 6:35 to work it troubled me
like the decal on my secretary's desk
that smiles on everyone the same
meaningless greeting or good-bye.
Clearly the pumpkin no longer believes itself.
It grins each day with less conviction.
It has taken stock of our futures as if to say,
Have nightmares, have sickness, have nothing.
I know I should cart it out with the trash,
but I am morbidly curious or compassionate,
O memento mori, my lantern, my life!

INSTRUMENTS

Teach me, dearest, poor dead one.
Had I known I would have tried to love you
down from your blind, beloved sky,
made you practice your favorite Schumann
where you stumbled, where poor dead
Pierrot stumbles, on the syncopations.

No piano or lover could keep her
from climbing into clouds,
the handsome cumulus,
its instrument-baffling breath.
Flying, she said,
is like having an affair.

Chandelle, Cuban eight, roll and split S.
No way out of the flat spin
she left herself in.
Nothing left but music on a spool.
Nothing of her beautiful, awkward self.
Nothing but the Steinway for someone else.

The satin dresses you wore at recitals,
for someone else.
A daughter too young to remember you,
for someone else.
A few odd lovers,
all for someone else.

But her poor lost self for no one,
for a few hundred hours in a pilot's log,
for the final flight plan,
the unrecorded arrival
in a shower of ice
near Waterloo, or was it What Cheer?

I will not forgive.
She should have practiced scales
instead of takeoffs and landings.
She should have grounded here
where she belonged,
so cool, so perfectly tactical.

I never learned anything well,
but now on cloudy afternoons
I practice Bach as best I can—
the first and simplest Preludes—
and try to remember what you said,
to play it slowly . . .

This morning, hearing jets
whine down toward Portland,
I remembered how I flew.
There was a narrow street
and old buildings and wires.
It was always chancy clearing the trees.

If you crashed you woke up.
I never made it, but now I think
I know what it's like.
You hover a little,
then go right up into the sky
where everything is clear.

And as you climb you leave
behind the little buildings,
the lighted window of a room,
a piano with one cracked key,
where a man sits beating the keyboard
for what he has learned.

I never met you but heard the story often
of the boots and wallet and the note
beside the chipper chute, no explanation,
no clue why you died with your boots off
as if you had merely gone to bed with blades
like a forty-foot hemlock chipped in seconds.
I imagine you were lonely or betrayed
or afflicted with some terminal illness—
who knows what?—or with the need to disappear
so completely no trace might improve
the claim of your absence.
Unable to cheat death you could at least
cheat those of us who make a living from it.
I do you a disservice then in writing this:

asking why you chose that way,
a brief red stain in a blur of chips,
riding the high-speed conveyer, poured
level to level, rising above us until
you dropped into the chip bin and from there
into the tall iron digester,
cooked with steam and caustic soda
and bleached white as an angel, unrecoverable
from the paper machine and the paper cutters,
reamed and packaged and sold—a rag-bond
reduction of your former self, for business,
for profit, for this present monstrous need
to scribble something out of nothing
and resurrect you, emptied from the page.

One afternoon a raccoon blundered into camp
wearing an overcoat of flies, its skull
and eye sockets sizzling with bluebottles.
It kept bumping into things, and each time
the flies rose in a cloud and settled
they pulsed with a blue electric light.

We'd heard of a mother bear nearby
and imagined her maternally murderous
in defense of cubs, the coon a curious
intruder raked beneath her paws.
What we needed was a gun I didn't have,
a bullet through the sightless skull,
and the trigger's merciful detachment.

Do something! you cried, as the coon
bumped against a post and the flies hissed.
Almost as if you had dared me,
I chose the stoutest stick I could and
struck three times through the fly squall
before its skull crunched.

On its side it ran, mouth and ears
oozing, legs pumping it nowhere, already dead.
I buried it, patting down the earth
where flies circled in empty, angry arcs.
A common casualty this one, no worse
than others left on highways
or caught in sprung steel.

But I could feel its bones crush
through my hands and see you writing

in your book, and thought of Leonardo
sketching corpses at the executions.
It seemed a metaphor for what
our marriage might become.

That day, the death you wrote of
was faceted with panes
like a rose window or compound eye.
I had a singleness that viewed one side
or else was blind to what you
saw and closed my eyes to every
blow I struck, every hurt.

What did you feel then, writing,
but the growing coldness, the first words
red with mutability and menace,
love, blood,
and the hands letting go.
Years my hands shook at the thought of it.

And only this morning, beginning this,
did it occur to me how sight
compounded could also divide us.
That all our lives it had measured us,
probing our common weaknesses
toward some final meretricious mistake.

One night, while a friend lay dying,
a raccoon came and stood on its hind legs
and scraped its paws against the bedroom door.
Get it out of here! he screamed until
his mother-in-law, armed with a broom,
drove it into the woods.

Days later, my friend died,
his lungs and liver eaten by cancer.
It must have seemed, masked and furtive,
like Hemingway's hyena, its breath
a darkness reeking closure.

What else make of this but some
commonplace coincidence of loss?
My friend is buried, my wife gone.
In his last letter he announced
his marriage, and his happiness
after a quick trip to Reno,
one of those twenty-four hour chapels,
the minister oily, not the kind
you'd buy anything from but the kind
who'd show up on your doorstep
with a valise and a hopeful smile.

I call it mercy, the way
my friends went gambling after,
counting their winnings from losses,
the years behind them, the weeks ahead.
The years they didn't have together,
a preparation; the years they won't,
the chips, the bits and bites of memory.
Words whose mercy they believed
in, a gathering, like my friend's
last to me: *I'll close for now.*
In haste, but with love, always, Ray.

FOR A FISHERMAN

Raymond Carver, 1938-1988

We were twice hurt because you left
and didn't tell us you were going.
You had your reasons: a book
to finish, a wish to avoid a series
of sorrowful leave-takings with
nothing else for anyone to say but
We're sorry, we love you, good-bye—
All perfectly understandable,
I guess, as your death is not.

If selfishness is wanting you here,
as a friend of ours believes,
then some of us are selfish.
You shouldn't have lied—however
right for you, it was wrong for us
who must go on living without you,
knowing how completely beyond
such obligation you are now.

This may seem formal,
as our friendship wasn't,
but the occasion demands it.
And I mustn't cheapen it
to fake a life gone on
in that happy way
you would have wished,
were you still here.

There is an absence in your wake.
All the anecdotes we tell
about you or the lines cast
after you can't wind you
back to us; they are life
support for us not you
who must remain distorted
in our thoughts like someone
under water, the self-made man
remade by us, no longer either
yourself or the way we knew you
when you shambled among us
hugely unpretentious
and hugged us to you.

Now in the harbor the buoy
we've named after you since you
rammed it twice by accident
without sinking, must toll
a warning of dangers
dead ahead or when we are dead
in the water as you were twice,
once from alcohol and
nine years later out of gas,
your bilges primed with fumes
from a rusted tank,
your boat a floating bomb.
Afterward I gave you
Chapman's *Piloting*.
It couldn't save you from the
crab that clawed your breath.

And if I mix my metaphors
with fact to address you
in this way and give you
presence to replace
what no longer exists
it's to reckon with myself
the cost, as the bell's
voice echoes from the water,
Come back, come back,
to fishermen still lost
at sea, unbuoyed by
wreathes cast yearly
on the tides and returned
as flotsam from the dead.

By heart we reckon you who
spoke so truthfully among
the usual fishermen's lies—
we listened and grew still.

One jewel of water on the tree
across the street catches light
and shimmers before it falls.
The light spreading from
one drop must penetrate
the soul and grow there until
the soul itself sheds light—
if you believe it.

I don't know what to believe.
Ever since your death
I've listened for your voice.
I've watched believing
you would signal us
if you could.
But there was nothing
until one night in a dream
you said, *You're not a poet,
your poetry's nothing!*
because I had not written
anything since your death.

I don't know if you were
speaking or if self-contempt
had caught your form and voice
and said the worst it could,
or if it was what I, without
cause, suspected you might have
thought when you were here,
you who gave encouragement
and love and believed that
words can seine us from
our shallow, hurtful selves.
You who wrote what you
had kept from us until
you were gone from us.

One jewel, one light
or the memory of it,
smashed against the brow
like a fist,
and this crude response,
oath in some brawl
of the self,
failing its subject,
as I failed you before,
cursing when you fouled
your line in my propeller,
and ashamed as I saw
the hurt like an oil slick
spread from my impatience.
Good friend, I didn't know
you had two years to live,
that four short years
would be the years we had
to fish the strait
your gravesite overlooks.

If I were Indian enough
I might believe that the
eagle circling as
your casket lowered
had come to ferry you
to some place where
the souls of spawned-out
salmon go, released
from flesh to stream
like consciousness
down rivers to the sea.
If I believed in the soul.

The next time you came
we talked and fished.
But the fish eluded us.
They were dream chinooks,
insubstantial as smoke.
When you complained,
We didn't catch shit!
I answered, laughing,
What did you expect,
being dead? Somehow
I knew this in my dream.
You laughed then as I
hoped you would, though
not loudly as in life.
It was a dream laugh,
illusive, a warning
not to expect too much.
Then, as if to tease,
you asked, *What do you*
imagine is the worst
I've ever done or said?
I waited for your answer
and was still waiting
when the alarm clock
rousted me from sleep.

This is all I know of
the afterlife, an after-image
like a light bulb,
its gray nimbus receding
when the light winks out.
And the word's light
still darker, graver
with its idea of light,
and of the soul, and
memory, that deceiver
we hook you with
so we can let you go.

~

MERLIN

And once out walking at night
I stumbled across the speckled body
of a small hawk,
the hasp of its wings closed.

One note, one note.

It sings in the rills between words,
between hopes.
It sleeps between leaves in a book,
gathers like dust on the piano.

I heard it once on a green hill
in Aberdeen in short puffs of wind
stirring the new grass among stones.
Prayer could not alter it

nor clods breaking upon bronze.

In some Havana of the heart I still
imagine my father, his broken English
explaining why that morning he left
he never looked back but went on
into his life. And was it a good life?
The last time I saw him was before
the war, on Christmas day. I was two,
watching the toy train he'd brought
slow down until, minutes after he left,
my mother wound it too tight and broke it.

I gave his name up for a stepfather's, but
whenever I thought of it, and I tried not to,
I hated him for leaving, for not writing.
I hadn't a photo, even, to tell what he had
looked like, only his shadow, and images
of trains. Later, in Klamath Falls,
my mother told me tales to scare me
from the tracks: horrible stories of hoboes
who tortured children, and of a kid with
both legs cut off at a crossing.
But nothing kept me away. On my tricycle
I watched the trains roar past, huge
Mallets, four-eight-eight-fours, with
pusher engines to scale the Siskiyous, until
my mother, missing me, switched me home,
pedaling and howling for my life.

In Seattle, uncle Andrew took me to the yard
to watch the engines shuttling boxcars.
And standing by the tracks, clutching his hand
as the switchers passed, bathing us in steam,
how could I know I wouldn't see him again, that
somewhere in the Ardennes a German mortar
round would fall behind the lines where
he stood drinking coffee beside his tank.
Mother, not his mother—though she had nurtured
him after my grandmother's religion tore the
family apart—hung a gold star in our window.
That Seattle morning's all I remember of him.
I can almost see his face, almost hear him,
mother's youngest brother, explaining
the complicated mechanisms of pistons
and drivers, of boilers and steam valves,
as the engines rumbled and huffed, bellowing
steam and smoke, their bells clanging.

And years later, a young man just broken up
with my fiancée, I took my grief to a river,
as I always had, and stood knee-deep
in the chill winter current, casting
toward a far bank where the steelhead lay,
their icy blue backs freckled with black,
their noses aimed upstream, fins sculling
in place. But nothing hit that day.
One by one they broke ranks to let my lure
drift past, then reclaimed their places.

I was almost ready to leave when I heard
the far whistle of a freight, one of the
last steam engines,
its carboniferous breath blooming beyond
a far curve of pinkish, bare alders
where the tracks followed the river,
then curved to cross a bridge upstream
from where I stood. Like soot, a flock
of crows started from the deep boom of
its drivers, the screech of trucks on rails,
the headlight, though it was almost noon,
swiveling its lizard's eye. And suddenly,
something, not nostalgia for trains,
or the woman who had left me, or my
father, or my uncle, caused my eyes to brim
and scald as they had once in St. Paul
when I leaned off an overpass to stare down
a passing engine's funnel and got an eyeful.

So tell me why, this late at night, I love
to hear that far hoot through the rain.
Why does it comfort me, when it's not steam
but air sounds the whistle, not coal
but diesel quakes the house and windows?
Tell me why so late in life, engine, father,
uncle, lover, your loss gathers to a sweetness
in one voice to sing a past more
perfect than it was.

Henry Carlile was born in San Francisco and grew up in the Pacific Northwest. He attended the University of Washington and since 1967 has taught at Portland State University. During 1978-80 he was a visiting lecturer in the Iowa Writers' Workshop. His first book, *The Rough-Hewn Table*, won a Devins Award in 1971. He is the recipient of Pushcart Prizes, *Crazyhorse* magazine's 1988 Poetry Award, and grants from the National Endowment for the Arts and the Ingram Merrill Foundation. He lives in Portland, Oregon.